Super...........

How to Beat Procrastination, Manage Your Time, and Double Your Output

GET MORE DONE.

By Patrick King
Social Interaction Specialist and
Conversation Coach
www.PatrickKingConsulting.com

Table of Contents

Superhuman Focus How to Beat Procrastination, Manage Your Time, and Double Your Output

Introduction

Many people experience cold feet (or abject fear) about quitting their day jobs and striking out on their own. It is, after all, a considerable financial risk and only becomes greater the older you get.

I, on the other hand, couldn't wait to take the leap.

The much-hyped ability to escape the 9-5 rat race and corporate grind was too appealing to me. I couldn't wait to start working on a beach with my laptop in one hand and a piña colada in the other. I'd seen it on Instagram so it had to be true.

The idea of having total freedom to set my own hours and work environment was so alluring that I ignored the potential downside.

You see, I used to be shackled to my desk for a prescribed period of time; it didn't matter whether I was productive, playing Minesweeper, or just twiddling my thumbs. My presence was the ticket, and the subsequent ride was boring and uninspiring. As long as I finished my assignments before their deadlines, I could collect my paycheck twice a month and clock out.

Most of my waking hours were spent in that stupor and it was beginning to feel like a poor use of my time.

I figured that by working for myself, I could make every minute count and work more efficiently by avoiding bureaucracy, bloated departments and pointless meetings. In theory, I would be able to do much more in far less time, and spend the rest of my time living my glorious life.

Those warm fuzzy feelings vanished when, two months after I'd taken the leap, I realized I had generated exactly *zero income*.

It turns out that to be productive you need structure and discipline – two things I discovered were not easily achievable on my own.

The exact freedom I cherished was the very thing that made productivity so difficult. Working on your own terms also means you are your sole source of motivation. This presents a problem when what you *really* want to do is go to the beach to play volleyball.

Without external motivation and no one to answer to, I was tasked with enforcing deadlines, defeating procrastination, and figuring out how to focus on the task at hand and just get stuff done... all on my own.

When I really needed to email a client back or calculate the numbers for my business expenses, I inevitably found something that needed to be scrubbed shiny and clean.

So out of necessity I started a period of research and self-experimentation to discover how to improve my productivity and output. Humans aren't innately motivated, so what means of external motivation could I create to push myself?

Many heaving sighs and late nights later, I had created personal systems that essentially guaranteed my productivity on a daily basis.

That's what Superhuman Focus is about.

I want to bring to you the wide range of productivity methods I experimented with to supercharge my output and efficiency and claw my business back into the black in record time. Some overlap and some conflict, but I used myself as a *human guinea pig* to discover exactly what combination of methods worked best and got me off my ass.

Sometimes the smallest tweaks yielded the greatest results, and methods that other people swore by just didn't resonate or had too great a learning curve. After all, the most effective method is one you'll actually use.

Each chapter represents a productivity method I personally used with great success to maximize my waking hours and ensure that I was working with a laser focus whenever possible. By using these methods, external deadlines and penalties to enforce my productivity were no longer necessary and my bottom line reflected that.

My output skyrocketed to record highs while working fewer hours because I was so much more efficient and focused on what my tasks were and how to maximize the time I spent completing them.

For entrepreneurs or small business owners, these skills are especially crucial because their time is so valuable in a quantifiable way.

There's not a person in the world that can't benefit from jumpstarting their productivity and punching out procrastination. You'll be surprised how great it feels to have that extra gear in your pocket.

Chapter 1. Kill Perfectionism

Perfection taken to an extreme degree has another name: Obsessive-compulsive disorder.

Yes, your perfectionism can be similarly unhealthy!

If you have to lock and unlock your doors five times before you can leave your house, it's no different than editing a document for the fifth and unnecessary time. It simply prevents you from doing what you want in a timely manner.

Defeating your perfectionist tendencies is one of the best things you can do to boost your productivity so that you get more done.

In your professional life, it's not expected and there are always buffers for a margin of error. In your personal life, because everyone makes mistakes of their own, the lack of perfection is almost always excusable. Perfection is not expected in any aspect of your life unless you're a surgeon performing an operation.

Everyone knows they make mistakes too, and they are in no position to judge you for something that isn't perfect. Everyone hits their own snags from time to time.

That's the first realization toward destroying perfectionism. Knowing that people accept imperfection is a big part of the mindset that will smash through your productivity goals and maximize your output. Your internal standards may be high, and you may be your own harshest critic, but the rest of the world does not operate on that rubric. So who are your perfectionist tendencies really serving? (You.) That leads to the second realization.

The second realization is that perfectionist tendencies typically manifest to protect ego and pride – to make sure you are as rejection-proof as possible and to prevent a hit to your self-esteem.

What I mean by this is that perfectionists are really people who are petrified by judgment. They feel that any error on their part will reflect poorly on them, and people will instantly cast judgment on their intellect or character. Thus, they leave as little to chance as possible by perfecting it.

They won't. So let it go.

For example, think of the last time you praised an artistic friend's painting. They probably rebuffed you with a self-deprecating statement about how they should have worked harder on painting the hand, but the painted hand looked perfectly hand-like to you. You couldn't even tell the difference between what you were seeing in the painting and your friend's standard of perfection. It made no difference to you whatsoever.

Your output is severely hampered when you waste time trying to *"get everything right."* Instead of producing fully, which the job or social situation might call for, you only produce a tiny fraction of what was expected or asked for.

Often, this tiny fraction is useless by itself, so you have just left a job incredibly incomplete by giving in to your perfectionist tendencies. What good are five perfectly decorated cupcakes when you were supposed to bring twenty? Who wins in that situation? Certainly not the 15 people who didn't get a cupcake – with or without sprinkles! And not you.

Perfectionism slows you down. By always looking back and double and triple checking your work, you are going to be moving at a snail's pace. At best, you produce a mere portion of what you should, and at worst, you are completely paralyzed by analysis paralysis and produce absolutely nothing.

Let's be clear that minimum standards do exist.

You can't expect to succeed with low quality writing, for example. But a cost benefit analysis must often be done to see what the optimal pairing of standards and speed is.

Perfectionism also destroys momentum, which is an *everyday superpower* that should be leveraged for maximum productivity and output. It takes a massive amount of effort just to begin any task and really get the ball rolling. When you can't let go of your perfectionism, you bring your momentum to a screeching halt. And it takes a tremendous amount of energy to get it going again.

In this sense, perfectionism is procrastination because it allows you to avoid future steps.

But have you ever just been *"in the zone?"* That's momentum, and that's almost certainly a result of letting go of perfectionism. It's when ideas are flowing from your brain to your hands or your keyboard and you aren't even thinking – you are just acting. Not everything you're doing is going to be perfect in that zone, but it doesn't matter because you just need to keep translating your thoughts into work or words!

Staying in perfectionist mode is incredibly inefficient. By definition, you are overly focused on getting every little detail correct. This means you're probably focusing on the *wrong* details, while larger issues are lurking and waiting for your attention. It's a very easy trap to fall into and even easier to get blindsided by.

It's not an easy thing to let go of, but attempt to focus on maximizing your output and on the bigger picture – because that's the real issue with perfectionists. They get caught up in the trees and lose sight of the forest, where the forest is the big picture goal they are working toward. Just realize there are diminishing returns on perfection, while the big picture goal will still be sitting there waiting.

Instead of expecting to do things completely right the first time around, focus instead on meeting your output goals. Once you overshoot your output goals, you can invest more time in increasing the overall average quality of your work.

Chapter 2. Create Daily Goals

If you've ever gone grocery shopping out of boredom instead of necessity, you probably filled up your shopping cart with impulse purchases and justified them with "Why not?"

How did you end up with marshmallows in December and nothing that could comprise a full meal? It's not like you're going to have a bonfire anytime soon, but, hey – *why not*?

When you attempt to accomplish something (even satisfying hunger) without a game plan (a shopping list) the results are often less than optimal. On the contrary, if you were to head to the grocery store with a list of five items, you would probably just grab those items and be on your way.

Why does this happen?

When you have a list of what your goals are, you create focus and don't allow yourself to deviate as much as you would without a list. It prevents your mind from wandering because it is set on a defined path which makes you more goal-oriented.

In the grocery store without a list, you wander up and down every aisle and are distracted by whatever catches your eye. Usually stuff you shouldn't be eating. In productivity without a list, you also wander around each different task and get distracted by whatever catches your eye. And then, when checkout time comes for both, you end up paying much more (in money and/or time) than you should!

To maximize your productivity and output, you can't allow yourself to wander around your desk or office aimlessly. You need to make sure you can stay focused on a daily basis.

Maximize your focus and productivity with a *daily goals checklist*. You can call this a to-do list, but I prefer the term "daily goals" because it emphasizes the need to constantly re-evaluate your priorities.

You might not be able to achieve all your goals that day, but you stand a pretty high chance because of the focus the list creates. Instead of freestyling, you'll face constant reminders of what your priorities are along with a semblance of structure.

Daily goals checklists keep you working toward your bigger goals while allowing you to tune everything else out, the latter of which is equally important.

What's the optimal way to create your daily goals checklist?

First, write your daily goals checklist the night before.

Start your day prepared to hit the ground running - don't make the mistake of working out your daily goals checklist in the morning.

Mornings are notoriously hazy and ambivalent, so before you realize it, you'll have spent an hour on your daily goals checklist while at the same time reading your emails. You'll also probably have a skewed sense of priorities because you'll fixate on tasks that are easier instead of those that are most important.

When you write your list the night before you'll have a clear and objective view of what you need to accomplish the next day, and you won't be influenced by the morning's inclination toward laziness and procrastination. You'll have the clarity of mind to properly think through what's truly important to do, and you will therefore prioritize your tasks accordingly.

Second, create a mixture of small, easy tasks, and large, tedious or difficult tasks.

We all have a finite amount of willpower and energy with which we start our days. This means we have to ration wisely to make sure we don't constantly feel as if we're slaying dragons. It's incredibly discouraging to finish a large task then instantly be faced with an even larger, more daunting one. You'll avoid the task and procrastinate, so sandwich your small tasks with large tasks. You can also substitute tasks you enjoy with those you detest – whatever method allows you to allocate your willpower effectively.

Those easy and enjoyable tasks also make good sense to start your day with because they will break the inertia in your brain and create momentum.

It's tough to want to start work when you're facing a few tasks that will each take hours to complete. Instead, start the day with something that is easy, or that you might even be excited about it.

It can even be a task that you've left partially unfinished from the day before – one that you can easily complete in the morning to get into the swing of productivity.

Third, daily goals checklists must be realistic, but they should also be aspirational and slightly out of reach.

Filling your list with *slightly* more than you normally would accomplish in a day can be extremely motivating and decrease the amount of procrastination you indulge in. It will push you every day and keep you racing to maximize your output.

Psychological studies show that the most effective goals are only slightly above your level because you can easily imagine their completion – you just need to increase your rate of speed. You'll create a bit of pressure for yourself and you'll enjoy a sense of achievement after you accomplish more than you thought you would or could.

First get everything onto a single page so you can then take a broader look at your priorities. The power of the list is its ability to organize your focus. And that's just the first step toward being a productivity machine.

Chapter 3. Write Everything Down

I hate *shower thoughts*.

Some of you know exactly what I mean. For the rest of you – a shower thought is a random stroke of genius that comes to you when you are inconveniently standing naked in the shower letting your mind wander.

And just like that, the majority of shower thoughts swirl down the drain in the moment it takes to reach for a towel – gone like a fart in the wind. I haven't found a solution to this conundrum other than using a dry-erase pen on the shower tile.

Where am I going with this?

Productivity is much more than maximizing output and crossing tasks off a list.

A big part of productivity is organizing your thoughts and ideas so you can remember them and efficiently implement them at a later time. We don't usually shut our brains off once we leave work, so when you have an idea that will pay dividends later, you *must take note of it* or it will disappear just like a shower thought.

Great ideas don't just fall into our laps (or stream from the showerhead). They come in a flash and are gone the next second.

It's unlikely that your memory banks will retain the particulars of a great idea for workplace efficiency in the midst of your excitement over a hot date or even what you are going to cook for dinner. If you fail to capture your ideas at the moment the present themselves, chances are great you will forget them and lose out on the potential flood of increased productivity.

Our memories are pretty unreliable; in fact studies show that eyewitness reports from memory are a terrible source of evidence in criminal trials.

The inspired idea in your mind gets pushed out by the mundane or the banal (or the hot date). It is easy to get caught up in the background noise of your daily activities and allow your truly inspired ideas to be quickly forgotten.

This is a simple chapter. *Write everything down*, even if you think it's not going to be important. Chances are what you write down will be a thread that will lead to another thread that may just lead to the answer you have been seeking for weeks.

If you want to maximize your productivity you also have to give yourself the tools that will enable you to capture your productivity boosting ideas.

For the more traditional folks, I suggest investing in a small notebook that you can carry in your pocket to constantly jot down your random ideas or reminders for tasks to complete later. I've said many times that if I lost my notebook, my life would be in chaos. Others, like notable author Robert Greene, use index cards for every idea they have, and file them away in a categorized shoebox.

For those who are more technologically inclined, I strongly suggest downloading some sort of notebook or Post-it app onto your phone to accomplish the same thing. It doesn't have to be anything complex, in fact, the simpler the better. It just has to be a blank canvas for your mind. If it's too complicated, you aren't as likely to use it effectively (or at all). So make it simple so you can use it quickly and easily.

Put real post-its around your house so you can jot ideas down in any room. Most smooth glass surfaces can double as a dry-erase board, so purchase dry-erase pens and place them close to any mirrors, windows, or glass doors.

When you're in the thick of a busy day, your mind doesn't turn off. Keep a running log of everything you write down with you at all times. You might be surprised at the small things that used to fall through the cracks in your life. It might be as simple as remembering to buy more milk, or as important as a key creative idea that will generate thousands of dollars for you.

Just make sure to date your entries and use notation and shorthand that you will recognize and understand later.

Here's what is currently scribbled in my notebook: the name of a painter I want to research, a potential date for a camping trip, a childhood memory that popped up from seeing a piece of candy, two potential book ideas, a quote I want to reflect on later, and the name of a documentary on a subject I am interested in. And that's just from yesterday.

It's best to organize your note taking into a few general categories such as work, home, friendships, significant other, and hobbies. Write in a stream of consciousness whatever you think of during the day and compile it all at night to see what you need to translate into goals for the next day or week.

This last part is key. Review and synthesize to make use of your flashes of genius. Write, ruminate, implement.

If you don't get into the habit of writing everything down, you are wasting some of the most inspirational moments of your life. By recording your thoughts, you can always come back to a previous moment of inspiration and come out with a working solution or implementation.

When you write down your thoughts, you're also exercising mentally. You are engaging in introspection and turning a mere idea into a process and analyzing the minutiae involved. The more you think, the more you analyze, the more you fit tasks together, the better thinker you will be. Constantly exercising your thinking skills will push your productivity levels up.

We can find inspiration for solutions in areas of our lives that are very different than the context in which the problem exists. A night out at a bar might provide insight into why your company's product isn't resonating with women, for example.

When you wake up hungover, wouldn't it be a nice surprise to have a note in your wallet describing what you saw, and exactly the solution you visualized?

The solutions to your problems can come to you in an instant. It would be a shame if you're not properly equipped to record these solutions. There's literally no cost to you – just the effort involved in cultivating a habit that *all* of history's greatest thinkers have practiced and excelled at.

Chapter 4: Create Public Accountability

New Year's resolutions are usually private – at least the real ones. People have no problem revealing the generic resolutions they don't feel particularly invested in, but they keep their real resolutions close to their hearts.

And accordingly, these are the annual promises that are made to be broken.

We might blame the hustle and bustle of the new quarter and everything it injects into our daily lives. When there are so many merging distractions and priorities, nine times out of ten, our goals and resolutions are the first casualty.

Sounds passable, but an equally large part of the puzzle is lack of accountability.

Most people's resolutions are personal and kept private. This happens for a variety of reasons, but the most prominent is that people can be highly embarrassed by their true resolutions and goals. They don't want to feel silly, marginalized, or judged.

But as long as we tell the *right* people – people with whom we feel safe and who won't judge us – having our goals out in the open can motivate us. It's part embarrassment, part not wanting to let people down, with a dash of making the resolution *real* by speaking it into existence.

In many cases, if we are only letting *ourselves* down, we do it too readily. It's often the easiest path through life and sometimes we can't help giving in that way; after all, nobody else is looking or being disappointed. It's okay to be lazy sometimes. We are experts at rationalizing and making excuses for ourselves but it will usually be detrimental to us.

It's why having a gym buddy is so effective – because if you don't go, you are letting someone else down. In the same way, it's why most people use personal trainers; people know the exercises they need to perform, they just need a degree of accountability to force themselves to perform.

When you make your goals public, this is precisely what's at stake.

When others assume you will achieve something, you will feel the pressure to do it. You (1) don't want people to change how they look at you because you failed to achieve your goals, and (2) you don't want to let others down if they also happen to depend on you to meet your goals. You can't continue to make excuses to other people the way you do to yourself because others are not so incentivized to believe you.

When you tell people you will reach certain goals and you fail to hit the mark, there's not a lot to feel good about there. You will look like a flake, procrastinator, and overall unreliable person. Those negative feelings are powerful motivators.

If you care a lot about what other people think, announcing your intentions will be a powerful disincentive to slack off. You will be forced to stick to your daily goals so you can hit your objectives and not feel embarrassed. Social and peer pressure can sometimes work to your great benefit.

Even if you *don't* care too much about what other people think, making your goals known can still serve as a powerful incentive because you won't want to let *yourself* down and fall short of your potential. Again, once you speak something into existence, it's more difficult to make excuses for yourself if you fail to accomplish it.

If you are without public accountability, chances are you will let yourself off easy and settle for mediocrity. But if there is an objective third party judge of your success, you will be pushed to meet those expectations.

In other words, there's a consequence to what you're doing or not doing. This is the big problem with most New Year's resolutions. People don't really feel there's a consequence for abandoning their resolutions. Not surprisingly, most people fail to stick to their resolutions and achieve their goals.

Take the example of setting a resolution to lose 30 pounds by a certain date.

You can decide not to tell anyone, and therefore not care when you decide to sleep instead of jog or eat a hamburger instead of kale and quinoa. The only person you're hurting is yourself and we're often all too happy to do that.

How might the outcome change if you were to tell five of your closest friends your resolution? What about posting it on social media where you potentially reach hundreds of people? What about taking the additional step of asking them to check in on your progress?

As the days go by and people ask you about your weight loss goals, you will start feeling the pressure. You are pushed to go to the gym more often. You are pushed to eat healthier. You cannot rely on your excuses any longer. If you don't feel pressure, you will, at the very least, stare reminders in the face every day, which can also have a powerful motivating effect.

Whatever the overarching reason, the progress on your goals will be made by external forces. This may seem unhealthy, but external forces are how we internalize any habit at the outset, so it's an entirely natural process.

You can use this same process of creating public accountability for any goal, task, item, or objective you want to achieve. Once the cat is out of the bag on even a routine, daily task such as sending out more emails, you will feel the same external forces pushing you toward productivity and focus.

What matters is that you eventually achieve your goals... and being accountable to other people is a great motivator.

Chapter 5. Batch Tasks

Henry Ford, founder of Ford Motor Company, got a lot of things right about cars.

He had a few competitors back in the day, but a primary reason those names are essentially lost in time is because he was also the creator of the *factory assembly line*.

On a factory assembly line, workers focus on one task at a time.

This streamlines a process and makes it far more efficient than having a single worker see a project through from start to finish, switching between multiple tasks. It allows workers to specialize and perfect their task, which cuts down on errors and makes troubleshooting far easier. For Ford, this made his automobile production efficiency and output shoot through the roof and dominate his market.

That, in essence, is what *batching* can do for you.

Batching is when you group similar tasks together to complete them all at once or closely following each other. Ford's assembly line was essentially 100% batching because his workers only performed one task – incredibly efficiently.

Let's take a common example we can all relate to – checking email.

If you have any sort of online presence or job, you probably have a steady stream of emails trickle (or gushing) into your inbox every hour. Constantly checking your email is an extremely inefficient use of time because it interrupts other tasks and scatters your focus whenever you receive a new email – many of us drop what we're doing to take care of something from an email. Then we have to start the original task over again because our flow and momentum has been interrupted.

Batching emails will considerably improve your productivity. An example of this would be to only check your emails at the top of every other hour. At first it might be difficult, but limiting your email checking in this way will allow you to focus on your tasks without constantly being distracted and having to re-acclimatize yourself.

Perhaps more important, it teaches the lesson that saying "no" to some tasks is just as important as saying "yes" to the correct ones.

Switching from task to task is a large mental burden because you are essentially stopping and starting from zero numerous times throughout the day. It takes a lot of energy to switch from task to task, and there are usually a few wasted minutes just regaining your bearings and figuring out the status of the task you were working on. And of course these kinds of interruptions only lead to achieving just a portion of what you can and want to.

In the example of checking email, batching allows you to stay in an email reading and composing mindset with all its associated skills, tasks, and reminders. Email catch-up is a distinctly different mode than designing a new graphic for an advertising campaign.

Batching allows you to save your mental energy for the tasks themselves, and not waste your energy on the process of switching back and forth between them.

What else can you batch? You can schedule all your meetings in one afternoon so you will have a free, uninterrupted morning to work. You can plan to do everything that requires computer access in the morning, and even batch parts of tasks such as the parts that require you to make phone calls.

You can also batch your distractions.

This isn't to distract and amuse yourself more efficiently – it's to make sure that you are conserving your energy and allowing your focused time to be exactly that – focused.

How can you batch distractions? For example, if you're burned out on a particular task, you might want to take a little social media break. By all means, take it!

But allot just a bit more time to check *all* of your accounts, ESPN, Refinery29, and whatever other distractions you occupy yourself with. Grab a new cup of coffee, take a brisk walk around the office, and say hello to your neighbor.

Get it all out of your system so that when you're back to work, you can have a solid and fixed block of time in which to focus. After all, if there is nothing new on your Facebook page, you will probably feel less compelled to check it. Once you knock yourself out doing all these distracting activities within the allotted time you can switch to productive work for the rest of your hour.

Some have referred to this as the *Pomodoro Technique.* A Pomodoro is a block of 30 minutes of time.

25 minutes of that time will be allotted to focused, hard work, while the remaining 5 minutes will be a

break. Once you complete 4 Pomodoros, you are allotted a large 20 minute break. It works the same way as batching distractions.

One of the biggest benefits of batching is that it prevents multitasking. Multitasking, as I will discuss in more detail later, is a huge productivity killer.

The more you divide your attention among different activities, the less productive you'll be. If you want to be more productive, focus instead on similar activities. When you begin doing something similar to the previous activity, you'll find it's much easier to get going because your mind is already geared toward doing a certain kind of task. Do all the similar tasks together, one after the other, and then move on to the next batch of similar or related activities.

Effective batching can skyrocket your productivity no matter the context.

Chapter 6: Positive Conditioning

I'm always amazed when I watch videos of dogs that can do countless tricks.

How were their owners able to train them so effectively? Are dogs smarter than we think? Are they truly man's best friend?

It's simple, actually. Their owners reward them with enough treats to make them fat. They use *positive conditioning* on them.

A dog will bend over backwards, crawl through mud, leap through hoops, walk on two legs, do flips, and run obstacle courses if you make it clear you will be rewarding them properly afterward. Dogs become highly motivated and focused when they know something they want is at stake.

Imagine a rabbit with a carrot tied in front of him. The rabbit can't reach the carrot, but keeps running faster and faster to get a bite of his favorite food.

We're not much different from animals. We function and focus far better if we have a clear goal and reward to work for.

Humans are creatures of incentives, and this is undeniable when we look at our daily actions. Everything we have and do is a reflection of the incentives we have and the reward we work toward. Whether our incentive is food, sex, social status, or money, we are driven by a perceived benefit or reward.

Knowing this, we can boost our daily productivity by setting conscious and definite rewards for ourselves to keep us focused. If we do it properly, we too can program ourselves to achieve amazing levels of productivity with simple rewards.

The first step is to define the rewards that will actually motivate you.

If you don't finish the task at hand, will you:

- Not get a snack?
- Not book your trip to Italy?
- Not get Chinese for dinner?
- Not hang out with that cutie?
- Not buy that shirt for yourself?

Once you have established the reward you will give yourself when you hit a certain benchmark of productivity, the second step is the **time frame**.

Set up a deadline for meeting the reward. Are you going to reward yourself hourly, daily, weekly, or monthly? Each period, of course, requires you hit a certain level of productivity or achieve certain results.

In many cases, you should set different tiers of rewards. For example, hourly achievements should garner smaller rewards (eating dinner at a more expensive restaurant) and daily achievements bigger rewards (going to the beach on the weekend). The biggest rewards should, of course, be reserved for hitting monthly goals (buying that new television you want).

If I want to buy myself a new television, I'm going to set a monthly achievement of 30,000 words written – 1,000 words every day. If I fall short of that mark, there are no consolation prizes. It's a binary process proposition: yes or no. On a daily basis, I'm only going to treat myself to a steak dinner if I write 2,000 words. Soon, writer's block magically fades as I'm motivated by something external.

When you associate putting in the necessary amount of work with your reward, you take away the stigma of tedious work and slowly associate it with a happy ending. Put a picture of Italy or Hawaii up right by your desk so you are constantly reminded of what you're working toward, and can positively motivate yourself.

There's a reason they call it work – I don't care whether you are a lawyer, a doctor, an accountant, or a dog trainer, certain parts of every job and task are a drag. When you use the power of positive conditioning through rewards, you short circuit this negative association, and the work becomes a means to a desired end.

Positive conditioning trains your mind to work toward a goal. Negative conditioning, on the other hand, trains your mind to run away from an adverse condition. You're running away from loss, embarrassment, or disappointment. Most people work better when they are encouraged to move toward an appealing goal rather than operating out of fear.

Feeling desperate can only achieve so much, and will additionally hamper your focus. By using positive conditioning, you engage the positive aspects of your personality.

In the end, it all boils down to what motivates you and having a clear view of what you're putting in all your work for. If you don't know what you're working for, then why would you work hard at all? It's like working at a job where you get the same compensation regardless of how hard you work. You go through the motions without direction or interest.

If your effort isn't tied to something that keeps you motivated, then your output is going to be severely hampered by indifference and lack of focus.

Positive conditioning brings out the eager dog in all of us!

Chapter 7. Break It Up

Very few people want to go to work when it's raining cats and dogs outside.

Me neither.

It's an enormous burden to overcome mentally. You'll get soaked, your shoes and socks will be puddles, and you'll be freezing from head to toe. Oh, and your only umbrella is broken. It's such a burden that you don't even want to go through the motions of getting dressed and putting on your boots. You feel defeated before you even get started.

Sometimes a horrendously rainy day can feel just like trying to be productive.

When we're faced with huge tasks that feel insurmountable, it's like looking through your window out at the rain. It's such an obstacle that everything feels impossible and pointless. We drag our feet, discourage ourselves, and bitterly complain the whole time.

But that's the wrong way to look at the tasks on our plates.

A singular, huge task such as "finish the 200-page report" can certainly sound imposing – if not impossible. But what if you were to break that monumental task up into tiny, individual, easy tasks that you can get to work on immediately? For example: preparing the template, finding the first three sources, creating a bibliography, outlining 500 words of the first section, and so on.

Otherwise, you're starting each day staring at the task equivalent of a rainy day.

One of the biggest hurdles to productivity is to look at tasks as huge, inseparable boulders. It's intimidating and discouraging, and when those emotions arise, it's tough to avoid procrastinating because tackling a boulder is a tough sell.

Unfortunately, this is a habit that plagues most people. They see only massive boulders and allow themselves to get emotionally thrown off track.

Break up your big tasks into smaller tasks, and keep repeating until the tasks you have before you are so easy you can do them immediately within a few minutes. Create small, manageable chunks that will be psychologically uplifting and acceptable and you'll kick your production up instantly.

Productivity is nothing without action, and action is much easier with something simple and easy to warm up with. Small steps can take you to the top of the hill, and let you roll down the other side to seize momentum. They help you break the inertia that leads you to passivity and inaction.

When you can knock out any task, you create more confidence in yourself to tackle the bigger tasks. You feel more at ease and your mind is imbued with the knowledge and confidence that you've already done quite a bit, so the rest won't be a problem.

Create small victories for yourself and think manageable and immediate. Trying to wrap your mind around a boulder only freezes your mind up and creates analysis paralysis because you just won't have any idea of where to start.

When you look at the big stuff, your first thought is that it's too tough, impossible, or highly unpleasant. Small chunks are easy to visualize and imagine doing, which means half the battle is already won.

Let's take an example that we're all familiar with — working out. You want to lose 100 pounds, a hefty goal.

If you go into the gym every day thinking that you want to lose 100 pounds, you're probably going to fail. It's a huge, enormous boulder of a goal. It might sound grand to proclaim, but in reality, it is going to be very hard to stick to because of how unbelievable it sounds.

You won't see much progress on a daily or even weekly basis, and you will understandably become discouraged. It's too much to face at once, like the rainy day from the beginning of the chapter.

But what if you approached your weight loss goal by breaking it into small, manageable increments (goals) and tasks?

This might look something like setting a reasonable weekly weight loss goal, creating daily goals of eating specific foods (and not eating others), and drinking water every hour. Eat 100 fewer calories a meal. Go on walks after each meal.

If you hit your weekly weight loss goal and successfully drink water every hour, it is far easier to stay motivated and focused. Meeting your smaller, weekly goal will give you a sense of accomplishment whereas making an insignificant dent in your total goal (100 pounds) will only make you feel discouraged and as if the task ahead is too great to achieve.

These are small tasks that, if done consistently and correctly, will lead to your overall goal of losing 100 pounds.

The emphasis here is on accomplishing small and immediate tasks and goals; these small victories will encourage and motivate you. Always seek to break your tasks up into smaller components, even if when the entire task is normal or small-sized to begin with.

Don't underestimate the power of a small victory.

Chapter 8: Productive Mornings

Humans are creatures of habit and routine.

In some order: wake up, brush your teeth, sit on the porcelain throne, and get dressed.

Your morning sets the tone for your entire day, so what can you add to that morning routine that will jumpstart your day and let you focus on what you need to focus on?

We all know how easy it is to zone out in the morning and lose literally hours of your day by aimlessly browsing the Internet. In the morning, because we're usually tired, it's too easy for the inertia of non-productivity to grab hold of us. Even if we're at work, sometimes it takes a couple of hours to get into the swing of the day's tasks and goals. It can be after lunch before you're feeling ready to dive into something big.

This is clearly what we're trying to avoid in this book. How can you make your mornings more productive, have greater output, and have less procrastination?

Create a productive morning routine for yourself.

Your best productivity starts when you have clearly defined goals – and why not have those goals and a proper mindset in place the minute you wake up? After you buy into the morning productivity routine, you'll find that it will become instinct for you to do productive acts when you wake up, which will transition naturally into accomplishing bigger and bigger tasks.

Instead of clicking aimlessly on random websites, you will gradually begin to click over to your tasks and action items.

So what's on this morning's productivity routine?

It's a fixed checklist that doesn't deviate in order.

1. Wake up. Don't hit the snooze button. Don't you *dare*.

2. Check the daily goals checklist you created the night before, the one we talked about in Chapter 2. Reviewing your list will immediately let you know what's on the docket for the day so you can start thinking about how to tackle it.

o 5 minutes.

3. NO SOCIAL MEDIA, NO EMAILS YET. Don't let these distractions cloud the priorities you carefully laid out the night before. These can also be incredibly distracting in the morning, so save what would otherwise be a wasted hour and leave the social media for a break later in the day.

4. Bathroom routines – cleaning, grooming, relieving. It is many people's first urge to do this, but I implore you to reconsider. If you can program yourself to hold off on these essentials until after you look at your daily goals checklist... then the daily goals checklist becomes essential as well. Ruminate on your goals while you're going through this part of your routine.
   o 10 minutes.

5. Get started on a relatively sizeable task. This is key to do before breakfast or coffee. You're seizing the momentum you experienced when you looked at your daily goals checklist, and starting it before breakfast will keep your breakfast short and focused. Often, this will drive you to keep working on it during breakfast as well.
   o 20 minutes.

6. Breakfast. Make sure you already know what you're going to prepare so you don't waste time trying to cobble something together from the

contents of your fridge! It's a good idea to have the same thing for breakfast every morning so you don't need to devote any brainpower to it. Instead, reserve your mind for thinking about how you will approach that sizeable task on your list.

- o 15 minutes.

7. Check your emails. Yes, finally, check your emails and reply to the most urgent. I've waited until this point to include this because otherwise, you risk getting dangerously de-railed from the other priorities you set the night before. You might have an urgent matter or two in there, but nothing that can't wait an hour.

- o 20 minutes.

8. Re-evaluate your daily goals checklist after seeing if there are any urgent matters in your emails.

- o 5 minutes.

9. Goof around. Indulge yourself a little bit to raise your mood for the upcoming productive day… but only after you've started the ball rolling on multiple fronts! This will naturally discourage you from goofing around and you might even begin to skip this part of the routine.

- o 10 minutes.

As you can see, this morning routine will skyrocket your productivity by cutting the fat in your mornings and getting you right down to business. It sets the tone for the rest of your day.

When you are productive first thing in the morning, you'll end up producing a lot for the rest of the day. Research study after research study shows that your morning hours are your most productive. Don't let those opportunities pass you by.

Just as you should establish a routine for when you wake up, it's equally important to establish a routine for right before you go to bed.

The end of the day is a great time for reflecting on your daily level of productivity, and to properly build out your daily goals checklist for the next day. Your nightly routine shouldn't be too different from the morning one – just make sure your daily goals checklist is properly set, and that you have done something productive you can easily pick up again in the morning.

Mornings can be make-or-break in terms of your day's productivity, and which one they will be depends on whether you can seize the inherent momentum or not.

Don't let the potentially most productive hours of your day go to waste by hanging out at the breakfast table! Use the positive energy, imbue yourself with an active mindset, and smash through your day's goals.

Chapter 9: "Don't-Do" List

Everyone knows the value of the to-do list.

Even if you haven't read about it prior to this book, no doubt you've stumbled across tips elsewhere about using a to-do list to increase productivity.

My point is that everyone inherently *kind of* knows what they should be doing and when they need to do it by. The act of writing it down just helps remind them. This makes them more likely to do what they know they should be doing – more than if they didn't have such a list.

Granted, this is mostly common sense and not what you bought this book for.

Well here it is: not everyone knows what they *shouldn't* be doing.

Along with your to-do list, it's equally important to make a *don't-do list*.

Each day, we're faced with choosing tasks that will create the biggest impact for us and there are many hidden obstacles.

Again, we all know the obvious evils to avoid when trying to upgrade productivity: social media, goofing around on the Internet, watching The Bachelorette while trying to work, and learning to play the flute while reading.

It can be difficult to distinguish between real tasks and useless tasks, and it will require some hard thought on your part.

You need to fill your don't-do list with tasks that will sneakily steal your time and undermine your goals. These are tasks that are insignificant or a poor use of your time, tasks that don't help your bottom line, and tasks that have a serious case of diminishing returns the more you work on them.

If you continuously devote and waste your time on these tasks, your real priorities and goals will be left untouched.

Here's what you should put on your *don't*-do list:

First, tasks that are priorities, but you can't do anything about them at present because of external circumstances.

These are tasks that are important in one or many ways, but are waiting for feedback from others, or for underlying tasks to be completed first. So put these on your don't-do list because there is literally nothing you can do about them!

Don't spend your mental energy thinking about them. They'll still be there when you hear back from those other people. Just note that you are waiting to hear back from someone else and note the date on which you will need to follow-up if you haven't heard back. Then push these out of your mind because they're on someone else's to-do list, not yours.

You can also push things off your plate temporarily by clarifying and asking questions of other people – this puts the ball in their court to act and you can take that time to catch up on other matters.

Second, tasks that don't add value as far as your projects are concerned.

There are many small items that don't add to your bottom line and often these are trivial things – busy work. Can you delegate these, assign them to someone else, or even outsource them? Do they really require your time – in other words are they *worth* your time – and will anyone but you notice the difference if you delegate the task to someone else? By taking on the task yourself, are you getting stuck in the weeds of perfectionism?

You should spend your time on big tasks that move entire projects forward and not myopic, trivial tasks. Often these are useless tasks disguised as important ones such as selecting the paint color for the bike shed in the parking lot of the nuclear power plant you are building.

Third, include tasks that are current and ongoing, but will not benefit from additional work or attention paid to them.

These tasks suffer from diminishing returns.

These tasks are just a waste of energy because while they can still stand to improve (and is there anything that can't?), the amount of likely improvement will either not make a difference in the overall outcome or success, or will take a disproportionate amount of time and effort without making a significant dent.

For all intents and purposes, these tasks should be considered *done*. Don't waste your time on them, and don't fall into the trap of considering them a priority. Once you finish everything else on your plate, you can then evaluate how much time you want to devote to polishing something.

If the task is at 90% of the quality you need it to be, it's time to look around at what else needs your attention to bring it from 0% to 90%. In other words, it's far more helpful to have three tasks completed at 80% quality versus one task at 100% quality.

When you consciously avoid the items on your don't-do list, you keep yourself focused and streamlined. You don't waste energy or time, and your daily output will increase dramatically.

Why read a menu with food items that are unavailable? It's pointless.

By preventing your energy level from being dissipated by those things that suck up your time and attention, a don't-do list enables you to take care of the important stuff first.

This can have a very dramatic and positive impact on your daily routine. The fewer things that tug on your mind the better – the kind of stress and anxiety they create only hampers or kills productivity.

A don't-do list will free your mind from the burden of having too many things in the air because it eliminates most of those things! You can focus on the balls that are still in flight, and steadily knock each one out.

Chapter 10. Diagnose Your Focus

Cut your losses.

The first time I heard that phrase was when I was dating my first girlfriend. I didn't quite know what my friends meant by it, but I didn't think it was positive.

It turned out they weren't fans of hers, and were telling me to cut my losses by not investing any more time or energy into a relationship they saw as doomed.

Cutting your losses means accepting a defeat or cost of some sort and making your peace with it before the defeat or cost grows even larger. Accept the current loss and leave the situation without trying to mitigate it or gain back what you've put into it.

It's exactly the same with productivity – sometimes you just have to know when to cut your losses and stop working, regardless of how little you've gotten done. Rarely will the extra few hours you spend "grinding" at the office be worth it if you're just not in the correct mindspace.

It's completely normal to lose steam or just not be in the mood for work from time to time. It's also impossible to jump from task to task at full pace with lots of energy. There's only so much work you can do in a day. There's a reason horror author Stephen King famously limits his writing time to 20 hours a week. He knows he will start to lose focus and the writing quality of his writing will suffer if he works beyond those 20 hours.

Once you recognize you're losing focus, it's best to stop working on a task at 50% capacity, take a break, and come back later at full 100% steam.

So knowing the point at which you lose focus is important, which is what is meant by the chapter title, Diagnose Your Focus.

By learning how to identify when you're losing focus, you can take counter measures that will boost your overall productivity or just smartly cut your losses for the day. The key to solving a problem is to first correctly identify it.

Different people get mentally fatigued in different ways. When you're mentally tired you stop focusing, you stop solving problems, and you stop creating. Instead, you're essentially just burning time and switching between tasks trying to find the easiest one to dive into. That's the first sign you should cut your losses – when you keep refreshing your email to try to find something small and simple to do.

The second sign is when you are physically avoiding your work instruments, like your computer or notepad. You know you have lost focus when you are rearranging your desk or emptying your pencil sharpener. At that point, anything else becomes more attractive than actual work.

The third sign you are losing focus is when you are physically getting tired or sleepy. Your work is just not making it into your brain anymore, and anything you produce while in this state will essentially be gibberish. It's like when you fall asleep during a lecture and wake to find your notes have trailed off into unintelligible scribbles and then stopped altogether.

The fourth sign is when you read or do something once, then immediately read or do it again because it didn't register with you. This is the height of distraction because you can't even focus on a passage of 100 words without your mind wandering off somewhere else.

Learn how to recognize these signals because you can't solve a problem if you can't identify it. Everyone is different, and you'll have to examine your habits and behaviors.

This chapter is just a complicated way of saying that you shouldn't always try to push through tasks. When you do this, you are basically throwing gasoline on a raging fire of unproductivity. It's not going to solve anything. You've already lost focus and trying to waste your willpower in that state of mind is a bad use of resources. Instead, identify the signs that you have lost focus and take a break.

Don't work through it. You can't use brute force to get through everything.

When you learn how to identify the signals of lost focus, you can also find your most productive times.

Identify the times when you start playing poker on Facebook or doing other unproductive acts. When you see this happening, step away from your desk, walk around a little bit, drink some water, stretch or do some exercises, and clear your mind. Once you feel your energy level coming back, get back to work.

Sit back down and tackle the work you were doing before. If you find your focus has changed, then you have experienced merely a minor disruption. But, if your focus is still lacking, take a longer break so you can re-establish it.

Chapter 11. Distraction Blackouts

If you've ever lost your Wi-Fi connection while at work, you know it was one of the most productive days of your life.

Without Wi-Fi, you couldn't check Facebook, Twitter, reddit, Instagram… you couldn't even watch Netflix! In other words, you couldn't access any of your most beloved distractions.

This allowed you to focus on the task at hand - no matter how miserable you were – and you probably completed it in record time. You had literally no other choice but to work, so you got yourself in *the zone* and dealt with it.

This was an unintentional *distraction blackout* – a forced period of time where you have no choice but to ignore all your usual distractions. It's obvious that this will lead to high productivity and focus, so let's make it a habit to regularly schedule distraction blackouts.

All you need to do is block out an entire afternoon – at least three but no more than five hours – and deprive yourself of any other distractions so you are literally forced to work on a task. Turn your phone on silent (actually, turn it off) turn your Wi-Fi off, don't rearrange your desk or office, and don't you dare procrastinate otherwise. Sit in an empty room with a single desk and chair if you have to. Some people wear ear plugs.

The point of the distraction blackout is to force you into a zone where you have no choice but to work. I know it's hard; it may even be uncomfortable, but it is necessary.

You are put in a position where you have two choices – to sit there staring blankly and stupidly, wasting time, or to begrudgingly do something productive. It's the ultimate *I might as well* situation.

Once you're in the blackout, there's an additional level of productivity you can create by gamifying it. In other words, you can ramp up your productivity by competing against yourself during a distraction blackout.

First, give yourself ambitious objectives.

Make sure your list of objectives for that blackout is longer than you think you might be able to complete. If your blackout is going to be three hours, include what you think would amount to five hours of work. The reality is that what could be five hours of work *outside* a blackout may really only be three hours of distraction-free work. You'll be surprised what you can accomplish when you are in the zone. Create this game plan before the fact so can just reach for the next task as you finish your current one.

Second, compete against yourself.

Make it a game of accomplishment by measuring your output at the top of every hour.

You are racing against the clock and racing against yourself. Work is not inherently motivating, so say you plan to edit 20,000 words during a blackout. If you only edited 5,000 words the first hour, you'd better do at least 6,500 the next hour. Whatever you accomplished in the first hour (or day, or distraction blackout), try to top yourself in the next period. This will prove surprisingly addicting.

This will ramp up your efficiency like you can't imagine.

Finally, you should schedule your distraction blackouts for your most productive timeframe of the day.

You might notice that some parts of your day are always more productive than others. Some of us are night owls, while others are morning people. Most people naturally have peak performance hours when they are more alert and sharp no matter what the context. As a result, the work we produce is better and needs less editing during those periods.

For example, my optimal time to schedule a distraction blackout is late afternoon, or after dinner. I simply function better later in the day and perhaps don't fully wake up until then. It doesn't matter what I've done during the day before that period of time, I can produce more at 50% mental capacity during those time periods than 100% mental capacity earlier in the day most of the time.

Figuring out your peak productivity hours and combining them with distraction blackouts is a productivity double whammy. You'll be doubly focused and alert if you pair them together, and knock out tasks on your lists at a rate you've never worked at before.

Regardless of how long your peak productivity times are and where they are during your day, you need to take advantage of them. You don't want to waste this highly productive "sweet spot" playing video games or answering email. Talk about wasted resources! Instead, plan for maximum productivity during these times.

There is an extra benefit to a distraction blackout, and that is the level of deep thought you are able to devote to a single subject or topic. You're able to think about it beyond the primary concerns you normally only see in passing, and can think at the secondary and tertiary levels. You'll be able to visualize all the connections between topics and tasks in a new light, and your creativity will be awakened. I frequently come up with spontaneous ideas for improvements, new projects, and exploring things I'm thinking about or working on more deeply during a distraction blackout.

Chapter 12. Do First, Edit Later

There are a lot of sayings about writers and their profession.

The road to hell is paved with works-in-progress.

It ain't what you write, it's how you write it.

We are all apprentices in a craft where no one ever becomes a master.

And finally, my favorite:

Write drunk, edit sober.

But my second favorite, and the focus of this chapter, is this one:

Write first, edit later.

The overarching message is that you should finish everything you're writing (or doing – in other words, whatever your task may be) before you double check and spend time editing and revising it. This doesn't only apply to writers, though writing and writers are a helpful illustration.

If you're a writer and you try to make every word choice and phrase perfect, you'll probably be writing at the snail's pace of one page a day. But guess what? Your perfect prose isn't the reason people will be compelled to buy your book. And moreover, there *won't be a book to buy* if you write so slowly, get mired in the details, and don't ever complete the manuscript.

So what's the point?

Do first, edit later – this is a tactic that will skyrocket your productivity because it encourages you to push forward and get everything you can onto the page before getting bogged down by small details (and before some of your best ideas slip away while you're focusing on perfecting a sentence). Stay on target with the big picture goal and leave the details for when you have extra time.

It also encourages the maxim of *do first, think later*, which you will benefit from as well. Stop thinking and plotting before you put pen to paper and simply start writing. You'll get into the swing when you start doing it and find your momentum building. For writers, this means just start typing whatever comes to mind and let it snake to what you originally intended to write about. You'll have more material to play with in the end anyway.

How can this tactic apply in your life?

The simple truth with most of the tasks in our daily life is that having all of *something* is far more important than having 75% of something that has been edited to perfection. Having an entire task, batch, or paper done is always the primary goal. Don't lose sight of that by spending time tightening up your work before you have everything you need – completion is the goal.

Too many people mistake a well-edited task for productivity.

Here's a dose of reality: that's not what you're paid to do – you're getting paid for how much work you complete. A completed daily goals checklist has far more value than a well-edited fraction of that list.

If you're so preoccupied with editing a tiny portion of your work, you haven't really completed your work. You're getting paid for a complete batch regardless of how well polished a fraction of that batch is. The more you have in total, the more there is to edit.

The animating principle behind this productivity tip is that you need to take action *now* and focus on reflection later when you have the luxury of time. You are in a race against the clock. Finish what you have to finish, and *then* reflect on what you've done when you can look at all of it. This is where you can edit and polish. What's important is you get everything out of the way and taken care before you start tightening things up and perfecting them. That's what you do when you've completed your task.

If you're so focused on whipping everything into shape, it will take you a very long time to produce very little work. This is precisely the kind of situation you don't want to find yourself in. The world rewards productivity and results, not the effort or the process. There are no prizes for "almost" or second place.

I would even go so far as to say that output and productivity comes first and quality comes second. I'm not saying you should abandon the idea of producing quality work. But you should put things in proper perspective and *productivity comes first*.

No book (task) = no money (payoff) – no matter how beautiful your prose and vocabulary are.

Within the details, there are those that matter and those that simply do not. Sometimes you will get your best results by ignoring some details that aren't significant and just focusing on bigger tasks to completion.

To be more productive, you have to focus first on doing things. Ship things out. Take care of business.

Later, once you've finished what you need to finish, you can come back and increase the overall quality of the items you have completed.

Chapter 13. The Multitasking Myth

You know who I imagine would be great at multi-tasking?

An octopus with two heads. To multitask effectively, one literally needs two brains and eight hands.

Guess how many brains and hands we are short? It's just not within human capability to multitask effectively, no matter what you think or have been told. Numerous studies have shown that multitasking is almost always a case of juggling balls that don't need to be juggled (and not doing a very good job with any of them).

If you're serious about boosting your productivity and output, you need to stop believing the multitasking myth.

Multitasking is a big fat lie. You simply can't do more than one thing efficiently at a time, so don't try to split your minutes in different directions.

You can either do one thing well, or you can do three things very poorly.

Unfortunately, too many people believe in it, overestimate themselves, and suffer lousy productivity as a result.

The main reason multitasking is so appealing to so many people is they have inflated views of their capabilities.

Most people believe they're good at many things, including the mental clarity to constantly switch between tasks from minute to minute. There's a sense of denial regarding the need for setting time aside and truly focusing. Not surprisingly, their overall productivity levels tend to be far lower than they could be.

The human mind may be a very powerful organic machine, but it can only focus on one thing at a time. If you try to focus on many different things at the same time, and there are different moving components in each task, it's easy to get lost and confused.

You end up running around in circles with very little getting accomplished. You end up expending a lot of energy but with very little to show for it. Instead of making progress on one task, you'll make a fraction of progress on five tasks. In the process, you'll have to re-introduce yourself to the context and conventions of each task. By the time you want to switch to your next task, you've barely re-acquainted yourself and have to move on.

It's like speed dating – you only get to know each task a little bit, and you don't really have enough information to make any judgment calls. No sense of familiarity with the time you're given and similarly ineffectual results.

Multitasking is the antithesis of batching, which you'll remember from Chapter 5 is putting similar tasks together to work on them all at the same time. By focusing on one thing and knocking it out as soon as possible then moving on to the next item, you can explode your productivity.

The great thing about focusing on the one task ahead is that you're able to track your progress. You're able to know exactly where you are with regard to the completion of a task, and what still needs to be done.

When you are multitasking, it's very easy to get your wires crossed and lose track of what you've done, what you still need to do, and what has slipped through the cracks. As a result, you end up doing things over, and in many cases, producing low quality work.

It's one thing to believe that multitasking is a lie, but it's another to fully leverage that idea.

To increase your likelihood of getting more done by focusing on one task at a time, spend more time organizing. The day before you plan to work, come up with a solid to-do list where you're going to accomplish items in sequence. Put a lot of thought into the sequence because you're not going to deviate from it whatsoever. Resist the temptation to jump onto another task. Stay the course.

Let's take Bob.

Bob is on the phone, on his tablet, and on a computer. He gets an email that seems urgent, so he starts answering it while he's still talking on the phone. He completely loses track of the phone conversation, and the report he has pulled up on his computer will have to be completely re-read to be understood. It only took one call or email to completely throw Bob off track and for all of the things he was juggling to fall out of the air and land on his head.

It happens to the best of us. Just forget the myth of multitasking. Your various to-do lists are specifically designed to defeat it, so only look at the list once you're ready for the next task.

Chapter 14. Categorize Tasks

A straightforward to-do list can be just as unproductive as having nothing at all. It can make you spin your wheels, create anxiety, and cause more confusion than it should.

After finishing a task, you can very easily slip into the danger pit that arises when you are attempting to select your next task, creating a loss of focus. Just think about the uptick in efficiency you would create if you had to make 100 phone calls and you kept the phone to your ear between calls. Once you put the phone down, you'll inevitably find a reason to wander off before the next call.

This occurs if you only list every task you need to complete without priority or organization. If you've got a to-do list that simply lists 10 tasks, how do you know where to even start? Do you start from the top and work your way down to the bottom?

You can spend 10 minutes trying to make sense of your task landscape every time you glance at it, or you can use categories to effectively milk the most from your list.

A list for a list's sake doesn't accomplish everything you need it to in an efficient way, it only ensures you don't forget tasks. Break your list into categories that will let you know exactly how to spend each minute of your day.

Here are the five categories I suggest for your upgraded to-do list. They are ordered from top to bottom in terms of priority – because that's what matters. This is how you make sure to milk productivity out of every minute.

1. Immediate Attention. Check first.

Immediate attention – well, that's self-explanatory, isn't it?

These are the tasks that you must do that day or even hour. There might be deadlines associated with them, either internal or external.

Order tasks within this category from most urgent to least. This is the first category to address when you look at your to-do list – everything else for the day is just a bonus and nice to have. In fact, you should block everything else out until these items are completed because nothing else matters. Don't look at the other categories until your Immediate Attention items are done.

Within this category you should order the tasks from most urgent to least. This is where the essential work is and where you should focus your efforts.

For a teacher, Immediate Action items might be grading homework assignments or writing a test to be given the next day.

2. <u>In Progress.</u> Check second.

These are tasks you have been working on or that might be longer-term in nature.

They are not urgent. In Progress items are for all purposes and intents what you were planning to begin your day with, except for the fire drill of the Immediate Attention tasks.

You may not be able to finish them that day or hour, but you should check in to see how they are progressing *after* you've attended to your most urgent Immediate Attention items. These are also items that might need incremental work every day, so make sure to meet your daily responsibility to them.

These tasks won't make it into the Immediate Attention category because they can't be accomplished in one day or sitting, so their urgency is lower. Still, this should be the second category you check to make sure that long-term projects are indeed moving along as they should.

For a teacher, In Progress items might be monitoring grades, dealing with emails from parents, or organizing a field trip for next week.

3. <u>Follow-ups.</u> Check third.

These are items that aren't necessarily in your control, but you need to check up on them to make sure they are moving along. This category is outward-facing and focused on corresponding with others and checking on tasks in motion. Most of the time, your emails and calls can be pushed down to this level of priority.

Things you might list here are to remind others about something, to follow up on a project, or to call someone back. This is also where you take note of tasks about which you have not heard back.

This category is mainly for checking the progress of tasks that have made it out of the prior two categories – if they have been stalled on something unrelated to you, your job still isn't done yet!

Even so, these don't warrant a higher priority because the main focus isn't on you – you just want to make sure they will be ready for you when you need them.

For a teacher, Follow-up items might be making sure all permission slips have been signed and organizing a teacher's luncheon is on track.

4. Underline: Upcoming. Check fourth.

The Upcoming tasks are a category you want to keep your peripheral vision on.

These are things that might be tomorrow or next week, or they might depend on the current tasks you are finishing up now.

Whatever the case, they aren't things you should currently be devoting your time to. They are the next dominos to fall and what you should proactively plan for so you have a clear idea of what the rest of your week or month looks like.

It's a good idea to plan out your Upcoming tasks as far ahead of time as possible and simply be aware of what's going to be on your docket on any given day or week.

This ensures you don't miss anything by constantly thinking about what your next steps are. What will you need to focus on once your current docket is clear, and what kind of urgency will those items require once they become current?

This is the category of tasks that people can most stand to improve on. We all know what tasks are urgent and require our primary and secondary efforts, but what about what follows? Focusing more attention to this category will help you maintain better focus in the long run.

For a teacher, Upcoming items might be thinking ahead to group projects for the next unit and projecting when you will run out of construction paper.

5.   Ideas. Check last.

This category should resemble more of a list of ideas and tasks that you want to explore. They are aspirational. It might say something like "Phone as a memory recorder?" These are ideas that you can't devote time to immediately and are therefore your last priority. But you still need to keep them in mind.

Make your to-do list a place for you to take notes for formulating ideas for new tasks and projects. Take notes on your future projects whenever you can and they will take shape sooner rather than later. These ideas will often start as big picture tasks and then break down into small, manageable chunks and tasks.

This category is for the future and is not an immediate priority. If you have extra time, this is something you can work on developing, but not until the rest of the categories are accounted for – those are higher priorities to take care of and manage. Ideas is the last category you check.

For a teacher, Ideas items might be researching next year's curriculum and new ideas for class field trips.

Remember, the objective of categorizing your to-do list is to cut down on the mental energy required to sort your daily tasks.

If it takes you 5-10 minutes every time you look at your list to figure out which task to tackle next, that's a massive inefficiency that needs to change. If you institute categories, you'll know exactly what you should be doing at any minute of the day with just a quick glance.

Chapter 15. Protect Your Time

People are inherently selfish. They'll ask things of you and not offer to reciprocate, often thinking nothing of it. Of course, most people are relatively subtle about this or we would disown most of our friends.

The biggest way people subtly, and sometimes unknowingly, act selfish is when they monopolize your time.

When given the opportunity, many of your friends or co-workers will hog your time and leave little for your own tasks and interests.

It could be as simple as guilt-tripping you to come to an event, trapping you in conversations that are 100% about them, or inviting you for coffee to *"pick your brain."* These are all selfish motivations that you've likely wanted to avoid and find a way out of before.

To punch out procrastination and extend your focus, you need to take your time back from other people.

It's tough to say no to your friends, but if you spend all of your time doing things you feel obligated to do, people simply won't respect your time. They'll know they can have you there at a moment's notice, and they will take you for granted.

Luckily, you can do this in a very diplomatic way.

To make people respect your time, *make them act first*.

Instead of telling them no, create a *small hoop* that people have to jump through before you actually give them your time.

The best way I've managed to put this into practice is with a pre-meeting email or act. If someone wants an uninterrupted block of my time (that I'm not sure will benefit my productivity or overall output), I ask them to follow up with me via email about their concern or question *before* I actually meet with them. This puts the onus on someone else, and I am able to sit back and wait for them.

This also applies when people ask me to attend events I'm not so keen on – so you can use it in both your personal and professional life.

I've found this simple condition weeds out the majority of requests for my time simply because most people can't be bothered to send me the requested email about their question.

Well, if they can't be bothered to spend five minutes doing something for me, why would I spend an hour with them?

If they aren't willing to do that, then clearly it wasn't a burning question that would have led to a productive meeting. It would have been entirely for their benefit and a complete waste of my time while I waited for them to figure out what they really wanted to talk to me about.

So because this actually weeds out the majority of people who want to utilize my time, it's my diplomatic way of saying no. Even with most of the people who do actually send the pre-meeting email, I can answer their questions with a few written sentences and it saves both of our time... though especially mine because it forced them to accurately define their questions.

So out of 10 potential coffee meetings, 3 might actually follow up via email, and I'll be able to quickly and efficiently answer 2 out of those 3 questions via email. This turns 10 meetings into 1, which is a great win for your productivity and getting people to respect your time. I've also pinpointed the people I can really help in an in-depth way.

Now, it's not that I mind meeting with people who want help. I've had a lot of help along the way, and many of those same coffee meetings have been invaluable to my personal and professional growth. I love helping people whenever I can, but I simply can't afford to indulge everyone who wants to chat at the expense of my own daily output.

This is a book about maximizing your output, and these are the steps you must implement in your life to make the most of your every waking hour!

Applying a specific process to gaining actual face-time with you will make people aware that you are indeed busy. There are certainly times for meeting new people, but it's not when you're trying to maximize your productivity.

All you're doing is making people aware of the schedule you're working in. They can work their way into it – if they want to just hang out and indulge themselves, they have to do so outside of that schedule.

If people want something from you, they should be willing to work for it. It's more than just common courtesy, it's common sense. If you do someone a favor, they should put in 100% of the legwork possible and make it easy for you to complete.

Chapter 16. Beware Triviality

Parkinson's Law of Triviality is also known as the bike shed effect.

The story goes that there was a committee tasked with designing a nuclear power plant. This is obviously a large undertaking, so appropriate care had to be taken in addressing the safety mechanisms and environmental implications of building a new nuclear power plant.

The committee met regularly and was able to quell most safety and environmental concerns. They were even able to ensure the nuclear power plant had a pleasing aesthetic that would surely attract the best engineers.

However, as the committee met to deal with the remaining issues, one issue in particular kept popping up – the design of the bike shed for employees that commuted by bicycle.

The color, the signage, the materials used, and the type of bike rack to be used. The committee couldn't get past these details – details that were meaningless in the greater scope of a functioning nuclear power plant. They kept fixating on small, trivial features that were a matter of opinion and subjectivity.

Therein lies the essence of Parkinson's Law of Triviality – people are prone to overthinking and fixating on small details that don't matter in the grand scheme of a task, and they do so to the detriment of larger issues that have infinitely more importance. These are the tasks that, if you were to take a step back and evaluate, would compel you to ask *"Who the hell cares about this?"*

When you lack the clarity and focus to really tackle your big objectives, you start addressing tasks to fit your level of mental energy. You let your tasks run you. It's the classic case of not being able to see the forest for the trees and unwittingly keeping yourself from the finish line. This is especially pronounced when a group is collectively making a decision. Why?

There are two main reasons for this phenomenon.

The first reason is subconscious procrastination and avoidance.

When people want to procrastinate on an issue, often they try to remain productive by doing something that is perceived as productive. Trivial details are still details that need to be taken care of at some point, and they are things that we can tweak endlessly.

This is why we clean when we are putting off work. We're subconsciously avoiding the work, but making ourselves feel better by thinking, *"At least something productive got done!"*

Fixating on the trivial is the equivalent of cleaning the bathroom to avoid work – you are being productive in some way, but not in a way that aids your overall goal. That's why when the committee members were stuck on how to tackle all of the safety issues they defaulted to something they *could* theoretically solve – a bike shed.

Trivial tasks need to be addressed at some point, but you need to evaluate when you should actually address them. Triviality can easily sneak into our lives as a placebo for real productivity.

Second, and this refers more to group situations, the law of triviality may be the result of individuals who wish to contribute in any way they can, but find themselves unable to in all but the most trivial of matters. They're on the committee, but they don't have the knowledge or expertise to contribute to more significant issues.

But everyone can visualize a cheap, simple bicycle shed, so planning one can result in endless discussions because everyone involved wants to add a touch and show personal contribution. It's completely self-serving.

The main and only reason to call meetings is to solve big problems that require input from multiple people. Locking people in a room and letting them brainstorm is a fairly proven method for getting things done – *if* you have an agenda that you stick to. Anything else should be addressed independently; otherwise the level of discussion inevitably falls to the lowest common denominator in the room.

If somebody starts talking about something that's not on the agenda, you know that triviality is on your doorstep. If somebody is spinning his or her wheels regarding a tiny aspect of a larger project, triviality is already in the room. And if you find yourself suddenly compelled to organize your sock drawer while working on a particularly tough issue, triviality has made itself a cup of tea and is making itself comfortable.

Be on the lookout for these patterns – when you devolve into small tasks that may not need tweaking or do not impact your overall goal, it's time to take a break and recharge instead of pretending to be productive.

The key to combatting triviality is threefold: (1) have a strict agenda, whether it is your to-do list or calendar or other technique, so you know what you should focus on and what you should ignore, (2) know your overall goals for the day and constantly ask yourself if what you're doing is contributing to them or avoiding them, and (3) develop an awareness of when you're starting to lose energy so you can pre-empt triviality from occurring.

Knowing is half the battle when it comes to beating Parkinson's Law of Triviality.

Chapter 17. Time Is Opportunity

What's the most valuable possession you own?

It's not anything material – it's your time.

Time is the one asset that you will never be able to get back, make up for, or replace. Once the minute you spend reading this sentence passes, you'll never get it back. (But, of course, reading this sentence is a minute well spent.)

Time gives you *opportunity*.

Each new minute you're alive, you have the opportunity to do something. You can choose from an infinite number of choices. You can plan ahead, work on something, communicate with people, entertain yourself, or eat. There are so many possibilities when you have time at your disposal.

But once that block of time is gone, it's gone forever. You can't hop on a time machine and get it back. It is finite. You only get one bite of the apple – it's an

apple that we take for granted and don't maximize...
partially because we are sometimes unaware when
we are wasting it!

The sun won't always rise the next day and you don't
want to be asking yourself what you could have done
differently each day.

If you want to be happy with your life, make the best
use of your time. A significant part of this is not
squandering your time with choices that appear to be
necessary, but actually suck up your happiness and
opportunities.

Don't do things you feel obligated to do.

When you feel obligated to do something, that means
you don't see your own happiness or benefit in it. It is
solely for someone else's benefit, and it provides little
or no value for you.

Some might say it is selfless and giving, but remember
your own time is worth more than gold! So if you're
putting other people on a higher priority than
yourself, it will just lead to unhappiness and a sense of
waste.

If you feel there are other more important and
pressing things you should be doing, do those instead.
If you simply don't want to do something, don't do it.

Your most important goal in this life is to be happy. If you know you're not going to be happy doing something or going somewhere, evaluate where your priorities should lie.

If you have a task in front of you, and it doesn't lead to you being happier in the future, it's probably better to look for another task that will lead to a better outcome.

<u>Don't spend time with people whose company drags you down, or you don't enjoy.</u>

Negative people suck out your energy.

They are motivation vampires. In many cases, misery loves company. They are negative because they just want other people to be negative as well. They look at life as a horrible ordeal they just need to get through and nothing makes them happier than turning otherwise positive people into people like them.

It's poor for productivity and it's just poor for life.

Likewise, if you don't feel excited to see someone, it's a strong sign you could be using your time in a way that makes you happier and thus more productive.

<u>Outsource tasks that literally aren't worth your time.</u>

Depending on your location, you can hire a virtual assistant for as little as $2.50 USD per hour. There are research tasks, grunt work, and even work items that are simply a waste for you to spend time on when you have bigger ticket tasks in the wings. Small research tasks and grunt work can be completed by anyone, and having a virtual assistant take care of them for you allows you to literally work double-time and leverage someone else.

You can and should delegate larger tasks to free up your time as well, such as calling a plumber or landscaper so you don't have to use your time figuring those fields out. Your money should buy you free time and the opportunity to do with it what *you* want.

Maximize your leisure time.

Taking advantage of your time isn't all about maximizing your productivity or avoiding activities that don't add value to your life.

It's also about maximizing your leisure time, and making sure you enjoy the free time you do have in the way you want to enjoy it.

This means that instead of squandering an afternoon watching golf and snoozing on your couch, you should take note of your favorite activities and hobbies and proactively schedule them for your free time!

Since time is so important and precious, it's crucial that you value your time properly. You can boil this chapter down to the following questions to ask yourself when you prioritize your next week:

Does this make me happy or unhappy? Do I have a choice about whether to do it?

Valuing your time is the ultimate precursor to productivity.

Chapter 18. ABCDE Your Priorities

To-do lists aren't the best solution for some people.

Everyone processes tasks and priorities in different ways, so this shouldn't be a surprise.

Luckily, I've experimented extensively with a system of prioritizing your tasks that might be effectively used in conjunction with the rest of the principles in this book, or by itself. Categories, priorities, models – sometimes it just takes a different approach to resonate with different people.

It's called the ABCDE Priority List.

This method involves filtering your list in terms of pre-set priorities and consequences. This allows you to catalog your time and focus on the immediate priorities and making sure nothing slips through the cracks.

Just as important, it will also let you know what you *don't* need to worry about, so you can decrease your mental strain and focus on one thing at a time.

The ABCDE Priority List has five categories.

"A" = Very Important

An "A" task means the item is very important and needs to be done immediately. It is your first priority. You can't wait on others for this, and you're the only one that action depends on.

You *must* take care of it today and there are serious negative consequences if you fail to do so. It's a strict deadline that overrides any of the other tactics in this book – you simply need to get this done first or second.

Regardless of the stakes, there will be harm if you don't complete this "A" task. That's the easiest way to tell whether an item is truly very important or is a lower priority item. If your life will be negatively affected from failure to complete something that day, it belongs in the "A" category. This includes your own internal deadlines.

Urgency level: that hour or day.

Teacher example: writing a test that you will give later that day.

<u>"B" = Important</u>

In the "B" section of your priority list, you should include items that you *should* do that day.

Compare these with "A" items. "A" items are the things you *must* do. If you don't do them, there will be large negative consequences.

"B" tasks don't create consequences of that magnitude, which is how you differentiate "A" from "B" tasks. The consequences of not completing an "A" task might be catastrophic and unredeemable, whereas the consequences of not completing a "B" task might be fixable and minor in the long run.

It may be worth skipping over a "B" task solely to complete an "A" task – this fallout will be worth it for the greater good of the "A" task.

Incidentally, this is what separates "B" items from the rest of the hierarchy. There are still negative consequences with the failure to complete a "B" task, but there are none for "C", "D", and "E" tasks.

Following up with others and making sure things are on track to be completed or replied to are also "B" tasks.

Urgency level: After "A" tasks, whether at the end of the day or the next day.

Teacher example: give homework for that night and prepare lecture for the next day.

"C" = Nice To Do

In any priority list, there are always optional items you keep around just to make sure that you don't forget about them. Many people tend to confuse these items with the necessary tasks for the day, which makes this category all the more important.

As the category title says, these are tasks that would be *nice to do*. They aren't necessary for the day, and there is nothing riding on their completion. They're extra, and purely if you want to work ahead or start a new initiative.

They might bring secondary value to the other tasks you have, and they might position you for better opportunities in the future. "C" tasks aren't about the present – they are about thinking ahead and working for the future.

Having a good handle on "C" tasks is what will truly double your output. We all know our "A" and "B" tasks, but we rarely catalog what we should do with our extra time (besides relax).

For example, networking, sending cold emails, meeting with new potential business partners, and updating your resume are all "C" tasks. So are tasks that you've put off for longer periods of time like chores and taxes. They are future-facing.

There aren't any negative consequences if you don't do these things, just lost opportunities.

Urgency level: At the end of the day or whenever there is time during the week.

Teacher example: work on your curriculum for the next semester.

"D" = Delegate

These are the tasks you can delegate to co-workers, friends, or outsource completely.

Keep in mind that there is a big difference between delegation and outsourcing. With delegation means there are people working under you, or you have specialized divisions at your work that you can assign work to. Outsourcing, on the other hand, actually involves virtual assistants doing your job.

"D" tasks are things that you can assign to someone else. Often, they are tasks that *should* be taken care of by others and that you should let go of and trust someone else to do.

"D" tasks are often a waste of your time to do yourself. They can probably be done by somebody else at the same level of quality.

When you're faced with a "D" task, you must ask yourself if you would pay $X to be rid of it and not have to worry about it. Is your time worth more than the cost of having someone else do the task?

If you're not in a position to delegate or outsource these tasks, you might have to move them up in priority to just behind the "A" and "B" tasks. They need to be done, but not necessarily by you.

Teacher example: you can outsource or delegate decorating the classroom to the students themselves.

"E" = Eliminate

These are tasks that you should forget and take off your plate completely. This concept is similar to the "don't do" list.

You can eliminate more tasks than you think with zero negative consequences. In many cases, these tasks just weigh on your mind and may overwhelm you with a false sense of urgency and emotional stress.

Additionally, when they occupy space on your to-do list, you are unable to escape the mental strain associated with thinking about them.

What should you eliminate? Tasks that suffer from diminishing returns, that are already delegated, that are waiting for input from others, and that simply aren't necessary to your goals within the next month or two. File future aspirations away in a separate folder and keep them out of your daily field of vision.

Teacher example: detailed reports on each child's grasp of physical education.

The ABCDE Priority List is a method of making your life more streamlined and focused.

Chapter 19. The Pareto Principle

Back when I was starting my own business, I spent a lot of time spinning my wheels on tasks that didn't matter. This can spiral into perfectionism and analysis paralysis, and I was no exception.

Because I wanted everything I produced to impart as much value as possible, I spent an inordinate amount of time on small changes and edits that no one besides me would ever notice.

The overall message and effectiveness was largely the same, but I would re-work sentences over and over until I was satisfied with them.

Consequently, it took months to write and edit my first book.

This isn't to say that quality control isn't important. But I realize now there's no sense in agonizing over every word choice in a book, especially if the overall message and effectiveness will not change or be improved.

In the vast majority of cases, tinkering with the tiny won't make a difference.

The primary reason is the 80/20 rule, otherwise known as the Pareto Principle.

The Pareto Principle was named for an Italian economist who accurately noted that 80% of the real estate in Italy was owned by only 20% of the population. He began to wonder if the same kind of distribution applied to other aspects of life.

In fact, he was correct.

The Pareto Principle applies to everything about the human experience — our work, relationships, career, grades, hobbies, and interests. Time is your most precious asset, and the Pareto Principle allows you to use it more effectively for maximum rewards.

The Pareto Principle states that 80% of the results you want out of a task will be produced by 20% of your activities and efforts directed toward it.

In other words only 20% of the tasks you perform toward a certain goal will account for the vast majority of your results. Conversely, the remaining 80% of the tasks and effort are merely focused on bringing a task to perfection and optimal efficiency. They are mostly unnecessary in the name of high productivity and output and most of the time they are not worth the effort.

In concrete terms, 20% of the selling you do in any given month will produce 80% of your income, and the additional selling beyond that 20% has a serious case of diminishing returns. Often, you can produce results that are "good to great" on that 20% effort, and the time and expense needed to get to "amazing to perfect" is simply not worth it!

For example, if you set a goal of trying to lose weight, you will lose 80% of the weight by just doing 20% of the actions you think you should – eating within certain hours and hitting the gym three times a week. Everything else, like counting every calorie and lugging around Tupperware with broccoli and chicken – that's the 80% effort that will only create 20% of the results.

You would just focus on the actions that make the biggest impact and debate whether you want to even touch the others.

Seek the biggest bang for your buck. Details matter, but not as much as simply being present, in the moment, and on top of other things.

Lacking awareness of this phenomenon means you will continue to spin your wheels on 80% of the effort that doesn't impact your bottom line. You will also fail to identify the 20% of your business, tasks, or work that are truly working for you and miss a host of opportunities.

Acknowledging this principle can be seen as another way of avoiding perfectionism. To maximize your productivity and output, you need to realize there is a point at which working on something won't yield any more results. There's a point beyond which people won't notice the additional work or perfection, and where the purpose of the task is adequately satisfied. For most of us, this point is far earlier and lower than we might expect.

This additionally highlights the importance of simply completing a task – more often than not, it will be sufficient to produce adequate results whether you are 100% satisfied with it or not.

As for the remaining 80% of effort and tasks you may be able to skip... the first step is to identify exactly what they are.

What tasks do you *really* think people will or won't notice (even if you do)? What additional tasks might others tell you to just skip or disregard?

You'll be surprised by how much of the stuff you do day in and day out can actually be thrown away.

Now that you have knocked out the 80% that only produces 20% of your results, you can double down on the 20% of activities that account for the vast majority of your income and results. Devote more time to them and imagine how much more productivity you'll get if you can focus on what really matters in the core of your task!

Productivity is never about your intentions or how perfect you want to make something. It is purely results driven, and the Pareto Principle drives results in the most efficient manner possible by realizing the pitfalls of diminishing returns.

The 80/20 rule can give you the information you need to become more efficient. You can identify certain practices that will allow you to get the most out of your time.
And by clearly understanding how the 80/20 rule works, you can unleash your personal productivity so you can start getting the results you've been dreaming of for a long time.

Chapter 20. Manage Energy Not Time

Most people are worried about the amount of time they spend on their tasks and allotting enough time to finish everything they need to.

Time is finite, but you know what's even more finite? Our energy levels. We can have all the time in the world, but if we're fatigued or just unable to get "in the zone," you can consider that free time as good as wasted.

That's why it makes complete sense to be just as, if not more, aware of your energy levels and what drives them as opposed to simple time management.

We only have a finite amount of energy each day during which we can produce great work, so we must not let it go to waste.

The goal with managing your energy is to (1) identify when it is naturally high, (2) keep it as high as possible for as long as possible, and (3) take advantage of those times and avoid low-energy lulls.

How do you identify when your energy is at your highest and you are thus at your most alert and productive? Ignore all conventional advice about this topic because while many people have powerful morning routines, you might not fully wake up until 2:00PM, or later.

That's okay — what works for others won't necessarily work for you. Don't try to be someone you're not when your intuition tells you that mornings aren't for you.

The easiest and most effective way to identify your peak energy hours is to keep a short journal over a period of a few weeks (two to three weeks should be sufficient). In the journal, note the times during the day when you feel tired or lethargic and when you feel energetic or alert. When are you struggling to read the same page, and when does work just seem to flow out of your brain?

The common time periods are (1) early morning, (2) mid-morning, (3) post-lunch, (4) early evening, (5) post dinner, (6) pre-bedtime, and (7) night owl. Chances are you probably already have a clue of where you fit in, so there's no need for me to assign times to each period. Which of those seven periods suit you or fight you?

Finally, take note of how long these peak hours typically last. How long can you realistically maintain your focus in normal, everyday situations? How long will you need before you take a break to recharge your batteries, or simply call it a day?

Soon a clear pattern will emerge. You'll see with clarity when you have high energy levels and for how long. For example, my peak energy hours are nowhere close to the mornings. My peak time begins around 7:00PM and essentially extends until I get tired in anticipation for sleep. It lasts, with some variance, about five hours.

Now that we've identified our peak energy hours, how can we extend those hours and make the most of them?

The first step is to leave that space open in your daily schedule so you can utilize it to the fullest. Prioritize focus and productivity for your peak energy hours.

Second, eliminate your distractions and save all of your most taxing or brain-intensive tasks for that period of time.

If your peak hours are at night, spend the day taking care of simpler and less urgent tasks, as well as acts that you would use to procrastinate (like household chores or errands).

The activities you should save for your peak hours are the ones that are most draining to you. For example, if you are an introvert, then multiple conference calls will be draining. However, an extrovert might choose to take conference calls outside of their peak hours because speaking with others increases their energy and doesn't require their full concentration.

You may also want to make sure you only engage in low energy tasks prior to your peak hours, and if you aren't able to do that, recharge your energy throughout the day to keep it high by relaxing or playing.

Your peak hours are your game time. How does an athlete treat his or her body on game day, or how does a public speaker act differently on speech day?

An athlete stays off his or her feet as much as possible, rests, and clears his or her mind to make sure that they are in the moment when their time comes. A speaker does the same thing, except they rest their voice and try to speak as little as possible.

These performance-based people rest what they depend on; for the athlete it is the body, and for the speaker, the voice. In the same way, you need to rest your mind and utilize it as little as possible outside of your peak hours.

Third and finally, make sure that you can't make excuses not to work during your peak hours. Take care of all your distractions before your peak hours and make sure your friends know to leave you alone unless an emergency arises.

Planning your schedule around your energy levels is far more logical than planning around tasks. Your daily energy level is a constantly-running meter. Everything makes it run down and, accordingly, it is sometimes squandered. You have to keep your energy in reserve for when you need it, and not squander it on mind-numbing spreadsheets or emails you can answer in your sleep.

It's similar to willpower. The amount of willpower we have on a daily basis is finite, which is why it's easy to refuse a piece of chocolate once, but not for the seventh time.

And if you use all of your willpower and discipline to refuse chocolate, then you might not have enough left over for completing work or tasks that really matter.

A major theme in this chapter is that more hours worked does not equal better productivity or more output. Often when we spend hours upon hours on a task, we're not working on the task itself. We are fooling ourselves with busy work and procrastination.

Identifying and utilizing your peak hours to the fullest will allow you to do far more in far less time.

Chapter 21: Live In Your Calendar

I've extolled the virtues of to-do lists (with modifications) throughout this book, but it should be noted that there are numerous alternatives to these lists to increase your productivity.

The most effective tactic is the one you will use consistently, and it's been my aim to introduce you to a number of them so you can experiment and choose for yourself.

One of the prevailing opinions in productivity theories comes from the to-do list camp. The thinking is that once you have everything laid out in front of you, you can organize your priorities from there and make sure no stone is left unturned. The allure of the to-do list is to ensure that you are aware of the tasks, A to Z, for which you are responsible.

The other prevailing belief about productivity is to live in your calendar, as the title of this chapter states.

Instead of inputting your tasks into a static and context-less list, put them in your calendar.

When you put tasks in your calendar and plan them in concurrence with your actual day, you can also plan them based on how long they'll take and where you'll be physically. This way, you can account for literally every minute of your waking day and always know exactly what you should be doing.

So how do you live in your calendar?

Instead of having a separate to-do list, assign a time slot for each task you know you have for that day, and for each task you know you have during the week. There is an extra layer of thought involved because you have to account for where you'll be and what resources will be available to you. Do this the night before so you don't have to fiddle with it during the morning.

There are 168 hours in any given week, and once you fill in your calendar, you'll know exactly what you should be doing at each moment.

This is a relatively straightforward method. You are able to visually represent how long and complex each task is and get a far better sense for what you will be able to accomplish during the day and week. You'll know how to manage your time better, what's realistic, and how not to overcommit to people and work.

Arrange your calendar carefully every day and you won't have to debate what to do next. It's in your schedule. There's no decision to be made – it's in your schedule. Wondering what to prepare yourself for? Never fear – it's in your schedule.

Even if people use to-do list categories or ABCDE their priorities, they can still run into the beast of analysis paralysis – too little direction with too much choice. These are somewhat idealized versions of what you'd like to accomplish without the influence of your emotions, and to-do lists can be overwhelming and stressful.

Without a clear "DO THIS AT THIS TIME" arrow, you might still be wasting too much time in your day.

Deciding what task to handle at what time injects context as a factor and makes your choices far more justifiable and logical – and thus easy to follow through with. It completely eliminates decision fatigue in the middle of the day and allows you to just focus on one task, and then the next at the top of the hour. It's like a factory that just puts work in front of you, and you take care of it like a machine, which is with maximum efficiency and focus.

Having a calendar instantly puts you into the context of your day. That's the biggest weakness and downfall of the to-do list – the inability to forecast the setting of each task and take daily life into consideration.

You can consider your location, work setting, and energy level directly with the calendar method, something that is impossible to do with a simple to-do list, which is static and lives in a vacuum. All of your tasks, regardless of priority or urgency, look the same on a piece of paper. Nothing about the availability of time along with the non-work related tasks and appointments in our lives is addressed. Without this information, you may not be able to intelligently decide how to spend your time.

Living in your calendar, at least to some degree, allows you to project how much work you can take on, what your current capacity is, and when you can deliver. There's just something to be said for allotting a task a spot in your calendar – your calendar is finite while your to-do list is not.

Simply ask yourself: how many hours a day or week can you allot to something, and thus how many days or weeks will it take you to finish something? It's an exercise that few of us ever engage in, but can be paramount to your being perceived as reliable and trustworthy if you know when you can deliver and never take on tasks you can't account for.

Make sure to schedule your high priority items first, and then let the lower priority tasks fill in the spaces where they can. This is an instance of where your to-do list categories or your ABCDE identifications can integrate well with living in your calendar. It's just logical – if you had an important appointment with your doctor, you would block off the time for that and force everything else to accommodate it.

As a final best practice for living in your calendar, schedule your tasks for a slightly shorter period than you think they might take. If you think a task might take two hours, consider allotting yourself only 1:45 or 1:30 to get it done. Impose a deadline for yourself and create pressure not to fall behind in the calendar of your day.

It just might force you to work a bit quicker and more efficiently, and tune out your distractions in pursuit of staying on track in your calendar. After all, we tend to work a little quicker when our backs are against the wall, don't we?

Chapter 22. Focus Five

In this chapter, I'd like to present what I deem the *Focus Five* – five concepts about creating superhuman focus that didn't quite impact me enough to warrant an entire chapter, but nevertheless deserve discussion. An honorable mention chapter, if you will.

As I've mentioned, the most effective focus tactic is the one that suits your personality and that you will actually use, so the more you are exposed to, the more you can cram into your toolbox.

Whatever tactic you favor – to-do list, calendar, or furiously scribbling your tasks by quill pen on napkins – the following points can enhance it.

#1. Stay Positive

Or at the very least, stay neutral and grounded in your mood.

Staying positive is a force multiplier. That means the more positive you are, the better you will perform in all aspects of your life. Sleep and being adequately hydrated are similar force multipliers.

When you're absolutely positive, you tend to look on the bright side of matters and approach tasks with your glass half full. You'll set optimistic finish times, and strive to deliver early because you believe you can.

Positive people make the world their oyster and seize as much of it as they can. They see the light in every task, big and small, and can get through discouragement without a problem.

You may feel some bouts of stress, but they don't ruin your day or drastically alter your productivity whatsoever. You can deal and cope because you know life is a privilege.

Being negative invites stress and anxiety, which themselves are force multipliers. They cause you to doubt yourself, think pessimistically, and sour productivity.

Negativity makes you wonder what the point of anything at all is. You aren't eager to finish anything because you don't see the rewards as worthwhile.

There are also very real physical consequences of being stressed because when you are stressed, the amygdala in your brain releases cortisol which literally inhibits brain functionality. Think of how little you got done the last time you were in an angry haze.

It all boils down to the simple question of whether you can get more done if you've just eaten ice cream, or you are on the verge of tearing your hair out.

Relax and stay Zen whenever possible.

#2. Distinguish Creator Versus Manager Modes

This productivity tactic was very valuable in shaping how I organize my days.

Most of us split our time between two main functions: (1) creating (reports, documents, spreadsheets, designs, analyses) and (2) managing (organizing, coordinating, corresponding, emailing, calling, following up, monitoring).

It is often a struggle to mix and match these items on your to-do list or calendar because of the different approach each requires. Creating requires open-ended blocks of time where you are best left undisturbed. Managing is the polar opposite – you rely on strict punctuality and are interfacing with other people.

Creators are doing their best to avoid meetings, while for managers the meeting is their very objective.

For example, (creating) writing a report on a complicated immigration issue might take hours, so you just want to be left alone. But if you're (managing) supervising someone who is writing that report, you want to check in on them, correspond, and make sure all is in order.

They are diametrically opposing mindsets and many people find it difficult to switch between both modes.

The solution? Twofold.

First, know which mode you're in or want to be in, and let that dictate the amount of time you allocate to a task. One requires uninterrupted blocks of time, and the other requires access to other people.

Second, batch them – put all your managerial tasks together, in an afternoon for example, while allocating the mornings to uninterrupted time for creation. This allows you to let your mind roam free for some hours and also coordinate everything at once.

#3. Use Commitment Contracts

A commitment contract is exactly what it sounds like.

It's a contract you make with yourself, a friend, or a website (such as www.stickK.com) to ensure that you honor your commitment to a stated goal. If you don't uphold your end of the contract, you are punished.

This is otherwise known as negative reinforcement, and can be a very powerful motivator for many people. It is not for the faint of heart.

It's the modern day equivalent of being lashed for not obeying orders.

The first way to use a commitment contract is to (1) tell a friend your goal and *hard* time limit, (2) hand them a specified amount of money (I suggest no less than $100), and (3) create the condition that if you do not meet your goal by the specified time, your friend will donate your money to a charity that represents something you hate – no exceptions.

However, most commitment contracts between friends are easily shrugged off or let off the hook. That's why www.stickK.com comes in as the second method of using a commitment contract.

You create a commitment contract with a website that you cannot reason or plead with. You simply sign up, state your goal, deposit your money with the website, and start working.

You hit your goal or you lose your money, period. I can speak from personal experience that this just might be the most effective tactic of all. Machiavelli wasn't all wrong.

#4. Take Ten Minutes

When we're faced with the prospect of beginning something we'd rather avoid, it's all too easy to drop the task completely and procrastinate.

This *transfer time* between tasks is the most dangerous to your productivity and focus. It's a giant crack you can easily fall into for hours.

To combat this and jumpstart tasks you've been putting off or avoiding, institute a mandatory 10-minute minimum for anything you are struggling to do. You are going to do something immediately for at least 10 minutes. This will help you avoid procrastination, create momentum, and build your discipline and willpower.

For example, if you'd rather not do the dishes or your homework, that's exactly what you're going to do for at least 10 minutes. You can give yourself permission to quit after 10 measly minutes. Chances are you'll finish the task you were dreading, or eliminate the inertia that was holding you back and not want to stop after 10 minutes. Perfect.

The secret sauce is in immediate action. If you're able to cross this threshold, you'll see that the task itself is not so painful. It was just your sense of laziness and sloth that was holding you back.

You'll surprise yourself with how much more you can get done and how easy it is to build your sense of willpower. The difficult part is creating the snowball, but we all know what happens when you roll it down a hill.

#5. Change Your Scenery

If you've been sitting in the same cubicle all day, it can be easy for your mind to wander.

If I'm reading the same passage over and over, struggling for focus and comprehension, I simply pack up and change my scenery. To me, this is defined as changing everything in my line of sight. This might mean moving to another room, downstairs, upstairs, or to another office or café completely.

It never fails me. I'm instantly starting over with the same amount of focus I had when I arrived there. Changing your scenery will break up the monotony of your day and reinvigorate you. It will also essentially split your days into parts, where one part might be at home, the next part is at a café, and the next part is at the office.

This is significant because for most people, energy is contextual. This means that we have certain amounts of energy for each context. In other words, we have a separate gas tank for each piece of scenery we might find ourselves in.

That's why changing the scenery occasionally is so important. It takes advantage of the fact that you have compartmentalized energy, and you can become completely reinvigorated by simply altering your physical space.

Just think of changing your scenery like dinner and the subsequent dessert. Our stomachs have been proven to have separate satiety levels for different types of food – this means that even if you're full from the main course, you'll still be hungry for, and make room for, dessert.

Changing your scenery allows you to utilize all the tools you have at your disposal, tools you might not even be aware you have.

I tend to plan a few tasks for one location, another batch for another location, and still others for my home office. Obviously, you can only move to your next location when you finish your assigned tasks, so it will give you motivation to focus and complete them in record time. You've essentially created an additional incentive.

Beyond the psychological benefits, it breaks up the monotony of your day and wakes you up with physical activity.

Changing your scenery can reinvigorate your sense of focus by serving as a creative catalyst. You might be losing focus or becoming distracted because you are staring at the same "I Hate Mondays" cat poster, so seeing and hearing new sounds can help throw your brain into action. You can gain inspiration from hearing a song on the radio outside and instantly galvanize your sense of how to write your report.

You gain a fresh perspective to approach your work and all you needed was a breath of fresh air to manifest a breakthrough.

Chapter 23. Five Unusual Habits of Ultra-Productive People

I recently had the chance to interview Kevin Kruse, a New York Times bestselling author who interviewed hundreds of self-made millionaires and other high achievers. I asked him for some productivity habits he learned that people might not be aware of, and he graciously provided me with the following five habits.

Habit #1: Focus on minutes, not hours.

Average performers default to hours and half-hour blocks on their calendar. Highly successful people know there are 1,440 minutes in a 24-hour day and there is power in every minute. Most think of their day as a series of 15-minute blocks of time—they even change the default setting on their online calendar to reflect this. Most meetings, calls, and other tasks can be completed in these short sprints if everyone has the same mindset.

Habit #2: Focus on one thing.

Ultra productive people always know what their Most Important Task (MIT) is—that task that will lead them to their most important goal for the year. And they schedule one to two hours each morning to work on it, without interruptions.

Habit #3: Don't use to-do lists.

According to one study, only 41% of items on to-do lists are ever actually done. And all those undone items lead to stress and insomnia because of the Zeigarnik effect, which states that we fixate on incompleteness. Highly productive people skip the to-do list entirely and just put everything on their calendar, and work and live from that calendar. [Just as Chapter 21 states.]

Habit #4: Beat procrastination with time travel.

Your future self is often the enemy of your best self. That's because we are "time inconsistent." We buy veggies today because we think we'll eat healthy salads all week; then we throw out green rotting mush on Friday. What can you do *now* to make sure your future self does the right thing? Anticipate how you will self-sabotage in the future, and come up with a solution to defeat your future self.

Habit #5: Make it home for dinner.

As famed Intel CEO Andy Grove once wrote, "There is always more to be done, more that should be done, always more than can be done." Ultra-productive people know they will never actually be "done" so they might as well live a healthy well-balanced life and make it home for dinner every night.

Kevin Kruse is the bestselling author of *15 Secrets Successful People Know About Time Management: The Productivity Habits Of 7 Billionaires, 13 Olympic Athletes, 29 Straight-A Students, and 239 Entrepreneurs*.

Conclusion

So are you ready to double your output and punch out procrastination?

It's not an easy process to begin. Many of us have terrible habits ingrained in us from just getting by on our smarts and innate intelligence. But when the rubber meets the road and you have a deadline quickly approaching, we find we can't consistently rely on that anymore.

From a productivity and focus standpoint, you need a change.

Just remember a few things about the society we all reside in.

- It's merit-based.
- It's results-driven.
- And "almost" just doesn't cut it.

It doesn't matter how smart you think you are – it's all talk until you produce.

This is exactly why it's so important to truly learn focus and squeeze more out of your day than you ever thought possible. You could have a completely different life!

I've given you some of the best tools and mindsets that I know, and ones that have helped me launch my own business over the years. Take what you will and throw out the rest. I'll be damned if your focus isn't just a little bit more superhuman after reading this book!

Sincerely,

Patrick King

Social Interaction Specialist and Conversation Coach
www.PatrickKingConsulting.com

P.S. If you enjoyed this book, please don't be shy and drop me a line, leave a review, or both! I love reading feedback, and reviews are the lifeblood of Kindle books, so they are always welcome and greatly appreciated.

Other books by Patrick King include:

CHATTER: Small Talk, Charisma, and How to Talk to Anyone

Speaking and Coaching

Imagine going far beyond the contents of this book and dramatically improving the way you interact with the world and the relationships you'll build.

Are you interested in contacting Patrick for:

- A social skills workshop for your workplace
- Speaking engagements on the power of conversation and charisma
- Personalized social skills and conversation coaching

Patrick speaks around the world to help people improve their lives as a result of the power of building relationships with improved social skills. He is a recognized industry expert, bestselling author, and speaker.

To invite Patrick to speak at your next event or to inquire about coaching, get in touch directly through his website's contact form at http://www.PatrickKingConsulting.com/contact

Cheat Sheet

1. Kill Perfectionism

Realize that perfection is rarely noticed by anyone besides you (and consequently who you are doing it for), and your perfectionist tendencies can prevent you from simply completing your tasks – which is what actually matters in life.

2. Create Daily Goals

Write a daily goals checklist the night before so you can objectively examine what needs to be completed and what you should be focusing on.

3. Write Everything Down

Productivity can come as random inspiration, so make sure to always have something to take notes with to not let great ideas go to waste.

4. Create Public Accountability

If you create public awareness with your goals, you will feel pressure to complete them and embarrassment if you don't. This is a strong motivator.

6. Batch tasks

Group all similar tasks and interruptions together so you can spend your time on the tasks themselves instead of switching between them and continually re-orienting yourself.

6. Positive Conditioning.

Have clear rewards – both short and long-term – to adequately motivate your actions. Tie your efforts into a clear incentive that you create.

7. Break It Up

Look at large tasks as a collection of tiny ones, which are far more manageable to tackle and less daunting and discouraging.

8. Productive Mornings

After waking up, build a routine based on internalizing your daily goals checklist, starting a large task, and not checking your email until after you complete a task or two. Build momentum that will last throughout your day.

9. "Don't Do" List

Make sure to know what you shouldn't prioritize or devote any time to with a "don't do" list, which will boost your focus and decrease stress.

10. Diagnose Your Focus

Learn to diagnose when you are losing focus and you will know when to work and when to take a break. Brute force is highly overrated and breaks are underrated.

11. Distraction Blackouts

Block out hours at a time where you will just ignore everything else and focus on an ambitious task list. Once you're there, you can compete with yourself and make productivity a game.

12. Do First, Edit Later

Complete a task in its entirety first, then go back and revise it for maximum output and productivity.

13. The Multitasking Myth

You cannot multitask effectively. You are not the exception. Doing one task with high focus will beat three tasks with mediocre focus any day.

14. Categorize Tasks

If you split your to-do list into the following five categories, you will be far more organized and save time not having to debate which task comes next: immediate attention, in progress, follow-ups, upcoming, ideas.

15. Protect Your Time

Protect your time by screening people with a pre-meeting/call email. Put the burden of action on them to make them realize that your time is valuable. Be okay saying "No."

16. Beware Triviality

Avoid fixating on small ideas and details that don't matter in the grand scheme of a task. This is often a subtle sign of procrastination.

17. Time Is Opportunity

Time is the most valuable resource you will ever have. Therefore, don't spend it doing things you feel obligated to, pleasing others, or with people and things you simply don't enjoy.

18. ABCDE Your Priorities

A different take on how to best utilize a to-do list. Create categories based on priority level to effectively organize your day: very important, important, nice to do, delegate, eliminate.

19. The Pareto Principle

The initial 20% of effort you put into a task will yield 80% of the results from the task. Learn where the optimal balance is so you don't fall victim to unproductive diminishing returns. Also learn what is creating the most bang for the buck for you.

20. Manage Energy Not time

Your daily energy is far more finite than time available. Manage your time by knowing when you are naturally at your most alert and when you are in a natural lull.

21. Live In Your Calendar

Living in your calendar is scheduling all your tasks to 15 or 30-minute increments in your schedule. This allows you to account for context, energy levels, and location when you visualize your tasks.

22. Focus Five

Productivity is assisted with staying positive, distinguishing your creator versus manager roles, commitment contracts, taking ten minutes minimum, and changing your scenery.

23. Five Unusual Habits of Ultra-Productive People

Kevin Kruse details five productivity habits from countless interviews: focus on each individual minute, tune out everything but the current task, ditch to-do lists in favor of calendars, continually ask yourself how you want to be positioned in the future, and always make it home for dinner.

Made in the USA
San Bernardino, CA
10 December 2016